Do Lobsters Leap Waterfalls?

A Book About Animal Migration

by Laura Purdie Salas

illustrated by Todd Ouren

PICTURE WINDOW BOOKS
Minneapolis, Minnesota

Special thanks to our advisers for their expertise:

Zoological Society of San Diego
San Diego Zoo, San Diego, California

Susan Kesselring, M.A., Literacy Educator
Rosemount–Apple Valley–Eagan (Minnesota) School District

Editor: Christianne Jones
Designer: Nathan Gassman
Page Production: Melissa Kes
Creative Director: Keith Griffin
Editorial Director: Carol Jones
The illustrations in this book were created digitally.

Picture Window Books
5115 Excelsior Boulevard
Suite 232
Minneapolis, MN 55416
877-845-8392
www.picturewindowbooks.com

Printed in the United States of America.

Library of Congress Cataloging-in-Publication Data
Salas, Laura Purdie.
Do lobsters leap waterfalls? : a book about animal migration / by Laura Purdie Salas ;
illustrated by Todd Ouren.
p. cm. — (Animals all around)
Includes bibliographical references.
ISBN-13: 978-1-4048-2234-4 (hardcover)
ISBN-10: 1-4048-2234-8 (hardcover)
1. Animal migration—Juvenile literature. I. Ouren, Todd, ill. II. Title. III. Series.

QL759.S25 2007
591.56'8—dc22

2006003585

Editor's Note: There is often more than one species of each animal. The migration
habits described in this book are a general overview of each animal, unless a specific
species is noted.

Do lobsters leap waterfalls?

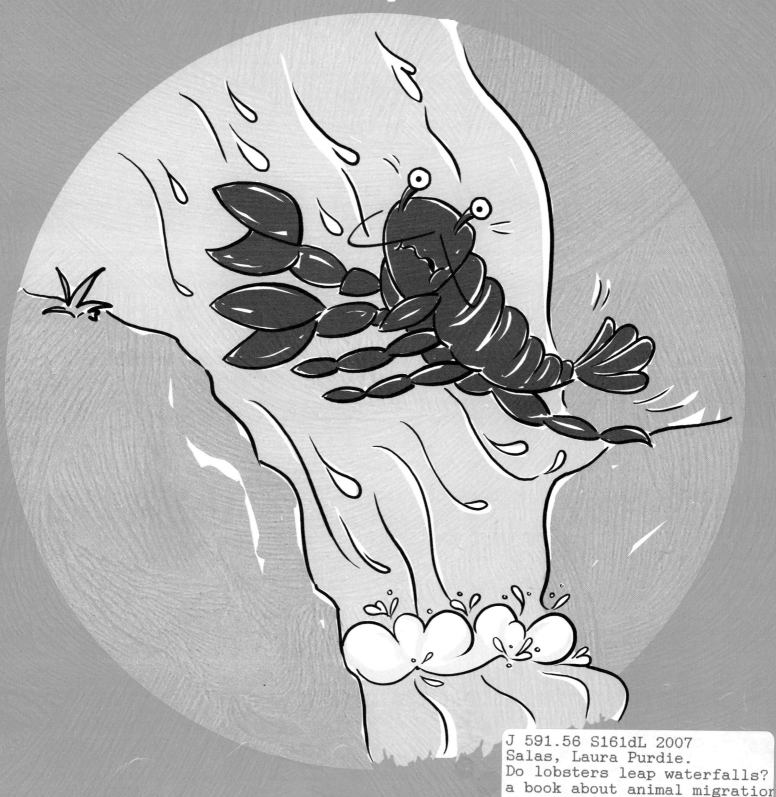

No! Salmon leap waterfalls.

Atlantic salmon hatch in rivers and float downstream to the Atlantic Ocean to find food. Then the salmon struggle back upstream and may jump up waterfalls to find calmer waters. Female salmon spawn, or lay eggs, in the same spot where they were born.

Do lobsters fly south for the winter?

No! Cranes fly south for the winter.

Sandhill cranes and many other kinds of birds fly south every winter. They sail toward warmer days and easier-to-find food. Sandhill cranes travel during the day and rest at night.

Do lobsters wiggle
deep in the dirt?

No! Earthworms wiggle deep in the dirt.

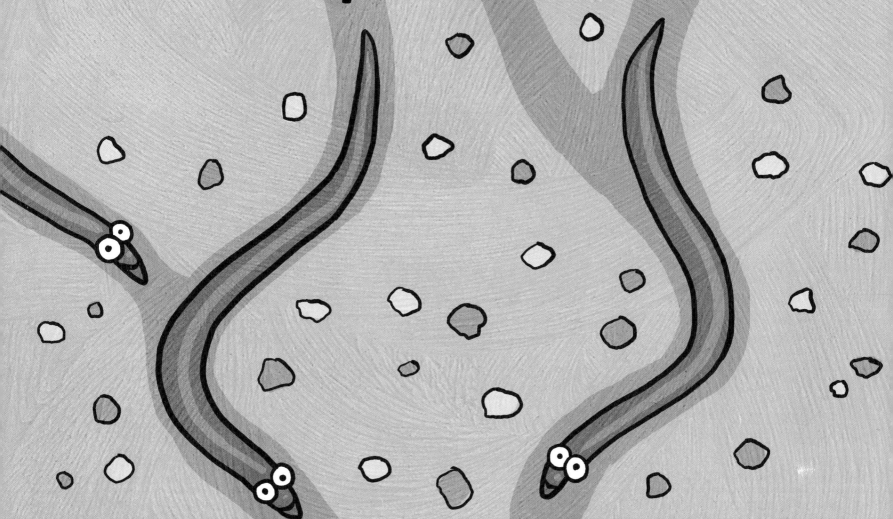

Earthworms migrate through the soil when the days turn cold. Each fall, they dig down until they are below the soil that freezes. When the ground warms in spring, earthworms tunnel up toward the surface again.

Do lobsters gracefully glide south?

No! Swallows gracefully glide south.

Huge flocks of barn swallows gather every fall to migrate. They speed south from Canada and the northern United States. Their feathers and forked tails flash in the sun. Swallows migrate thousands of miles to spend winters in warmer places.

Do lobsters swim to warmer water?

No! Whales swim to warmer water.

When winter approaches and the water cools, gray whales travel south from Alaska to Mexico. In December, the female whales give birth to their calves. In spring, the whale families begin their journey back home to Alaska.

Do lobsters move
to the mountains?

No! Caribou move to the mountains.

After spending the summer on grass-covered flatlands, caribou migrate north to the mountains. On mountain ledges, the wind blows the snow away. Caribou dig under the shallow snow to find grass to eat.

Do lobsters flutter to Mexico?

No! Butterflies flutter to Mexico.

In late summer, many monarch butterflies flutter, float, and fly from the northern United States to California or Mexico. That's a journey of about 2,000 miles (3,200 kilometers). It takes the next four generations of monarch butterflies to make their way back north.

Do lobsters run
across the plains?

No! Wildebeest run across the plains.

More than a million wildebeest move north across the African plains during the year. They are always on the move, looking for greener grass and better food. They move south, west, north, and then east on their dusty, circular journey every year.

Do lobsters fly around the world?

No! Terns fly around the world.

Every fall, Arctic terns leave the Arctic Circle to avoid the cold winter. During their long flight to Antarctica, they fly through summer weather. They enjoy summer in Antarctica and then fly back north to enjoy summer in the Arctic Circle. They fly nonstop for eight months!

Do lobsters march in a single-file line?

Yes! Lobsters march in a single-file line.

When storms pound the Atlantic Ocean in the fall, spiny lobsters migrate to deeper water to avoid the large waves. They push through the water in a single-file line on the ocean floor. Each lobster rests its antennae on the lobster in front of it for guidance.

Why Animals Migrate

Some animals migrate to stay warm.

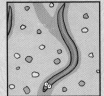 • • • • • • • • • Earthworms wiggle deeper in the soil.

Terns chase summer around the globe. • • • • • • • • • • • •

 • • • • • • • • • Cranes fly south to warmer weather.

Swallows fly south to warmer weather. • • • • • • • • • • • •

 • • • • • • • • • Butterflies flutter to California or Mexico.

Some animals migrate to find food or water.

 • • • • • • • • • Wildebeest move when the food runs out.

Caribou climb mountains to graze on windblown ledges. • • •

Some animals migrate to give birth.

 • • • • • • • • • Whales swim to Mexico to have calves.

Salmon struggle upstream to spawn. • • • • • • • • • • •

Some animals migrate for safety.

• • • • • • • • • Lobsters hide from storms in deeper water.

23

Glossary

antennae—feelers on a lobster's head used to sense touch and smells

downstream—the direction in which a river naturally moves

flatlands—areas with few hills, mountains, or valleys

forked—one end divided into two points

ledges—narrow strips of rock that stick out from a mountain

migrate—to move from one place to another

plains—flat, grassy lands with only a few trees

spawn—to lay eggs

upstream—the opposite direction in which a river naturally moves

To Learn More

At the Library

Bright, Michael. *Amazing Animal Journeys*. Brookfield, Conn.: Copper Beech, 2002.

Fowler, Allan. *Animals on the Move*. New York: Children's Press, 2000.

Huges, Monica. *Migration*. Chicago: Heinemann Library, 2004.

On the Web

FactHound offers a safe, fun way to find Internet sites related to this book. All of the sites on FactHound have been researched by our staff.

1. Visit *www.facthound.com*
2. Type in this special code for age-appropriate sites: 1404822348
3. Click on the FETCH IT button.

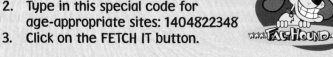

Your trusty FactHound will fetch the best sites for you!

Index

Look for all of the books in the Animals All Around series:

Do Bears Buzz? A Book About Animal Sounds
   1-4048-0100-6
Do Bees Make Butter? A Book About Things Animals Make
   1-4048-0288-6
Do Cows Eat Cake? A Book About What Animals Eat
   1-4048-0101-4
Do Crocodiles Dance? A Book About Animal Habits
   1-4048-2230-5
Do Dogs Make Dessert? A Book About How Animals Help Humans
   1-4048-0289-4
Do Ducks Live in the Desert? A Book About Where Animals Live
   1-4048-0290-8
Do Frogs Have Fur? A Book About Animal Coats and Coverings
   1-4048-0292-4
Do Goldfish Gallop? A Book About Animal Movement
   1-4048-0105-7
Do Lobsters Leap Waterfalls? A Book About Animal Migration
   1-4048-2234-8
Do Parrots Have Pillows? A Book About Where Animals Sleep
   1-4048-0104-9
Do Pelicans Sip Nectar? A Book About How Animals Eat
   1-4048-2233-X
Do Penguins Have Puppies? A Book About Animal Babies
   1-4048-0102-2
Do Polar Bears Snooze in Hollow trees? A Book About Animal Hibernation
   1-4048-2231-3
Do Salamanders Spit? A Book About How Animals Protect Themselves
   1-4048-0291-6
Do Squirrels Swarm? A Book About Animal Groups
   1-4048-0287-8
Do Turtles Sleep in Treetops? A Book About Animal Homes
   1-4048-2232-1
Do Whales Have Wings? A Book About Animal Bodies
   1-4048-0103-0
Does an Elephant Fit in Your Hand? A Book About Animal Sizes
   1-4048-2235-6